PERTURBED PEOPLE AND PROFANITY-

PERTURBED PEOPLE AND PROFANITY—

JON OLIVER & KATIE TONN

PACIFIC PRESS PUBLISHING ASSOCIATION
Mountain View, California
Oshawa, Ontario

Cover art and design by Cliff Rusch
Pacific Press Publishing Association
Mountain View, California
Oshawa, Ontario

Library of Congress Cataloging in Publication Data

Oliver, Jon, 1955—
   Perturbed people and profanity.

   1. Swearing.   I. Tonn, Katie, 1944—
II. Title.
BV4627.S9043   241'.3   81-619
ISBN 0-8163-0425-4   AACR2

Comic-strip captions—probably seen by each of us at one time or another. However conveyed, the words and symbols indicate profanity of some sort. Whether they are intended to denote obscenity, mere "social swearing," or a misuse of God's name is left to us to determine from the context of the prose or cartoon.

The use of profanity is much more common today than it was even twenty or thirty years ago. What our parents or grandparents would have uttered only in extreme instances (if ever) is now often heard from toddlers barely able to form sentences. When our parents and grandparents, in their youthful exuberance, were expressing their verbal freedom from their parents and grandparents, such words as *darn, doggone, tarnation, by gum,* etc., were considered pretty racy. Today much more graphic expletives are used by the younger set to express their verbal independence (so much so that one might think there was already an organized thrust for "children's lib" in this country).

It is almost impossible to live in today's society and not be confronted—and affected—by strongly descriptive profanity. We notice it in newspapers, magazines, current books, and films, on television and radio, on the campus, on the street and even in the business world.

Perhaps we should say, *especially* in the business world. Many of us, having taken a part- or full-time job, have had to face the scorching blast of seemingly nonstop profane vulgarity on a daily basis (an experience we may have been ill-prepared to handle if we had recently left a relatively protected church-affiliated school). After a period of time among persons in such a highly charged atmosphere, it is difficult to keep from using their phraseology. We are tempted to use it out of a sort of self-preserving reflection of our surroundings. The thought patterns begin, chameleonlike, to match those of the environment. Therefore, even those of us who are not practiced in profanity can run into the problem of echoing back someone else's speech without stopping to think about what we've said.

So, whether the color of our speech comes by choice or default, it is a good idea to try to understand why people use profanity and what it signifies in a person's life.

Now, some of us at this point would probably like to say, "I guess something like that *could* happen to me, too, so I'd better pay attention—" and thereby exclude themselves from any intentional involvement. We all need the "preacher" to set the record straight: "Your heart knows that many times you have yourself cursed others."[1]

You may not be one of the many people who seem to use profanity for the same apparent reason that some would climb a mountain— because it is there. But the use of profanity—

begun perhaps as a part of asserting grown-up independence—can become a seemingly convenient mode of expressing momentary anger, dismay, frustration, derision, or dislike. Then, too, it's all too easy sometimes to conclude that "everyone" uses it. We are social creatures and usually disdain to "stick out" by appearing too different from our peers. For this reason alone, many young people find themselves unthinkingly adopting various words or phrases which are considered by their elders to be shockingly profane.

On the other hand, mere familiarity brought about by daily contact can lead to the use of certain words because they just pop out (often at very inappropriate times) when they don't necessarily reflect *extreme* feelings at all. In every degree of usage, however, and especially in the severe case where nearly every sentence is liberally sprinkled with profanity, we need to search for some deeper influences than those just described.

The most reliable and relevant information to be found on the subject is contained in Scripture. As you might imagine, Bible authors do not take very kindly to profanity, cursing, swearing, and blasphemy. But why? As we pursue the answer, let's see how God's Word characterizes questionable talk and those who engage in its use. In his letter, James raises a red flag, warning us that there are issues involved which transcend those which meet the eye:

"Beasts and birds of every kind, creatures that crawl on the ground or swim in the sea, can be subdued and have been subdued by mankind; but no man can subdue the tongue. It is an intractable evil, charged with deadly venom. We use it to sing praises of our Lord and Father, and we use it to invoke curses upon our fellow-men who are made in God's likeness. Out of the same mouth come praises and curses."[2]

Something is wrong, James seems to say. Terribly wrong. How can the same mouth pour out both blessings and cursings? When fresh and salty water reach a pool, you don't continue to have both separately; the whole pond turns salty. How can we both bless God and curse men who are made in the image of God? It just doesn't follow to think that we can have both sweet and salty language—and yet we try.

Those authors who came before Christ's time were not silent on the subject either. Hosea pointed out long ago that profanity loves bad company—and not simply in terms of the kind of people it attracts. Take a look at this passage from Hosea's Old Testament prophecy:

"Hear the word of the Lord, O people of Israel; for the Lord has a controversy with the inhabitants of the land. There is no faithfulness or kindness, and no knowledge of God in the land; there is swearing, lying, killing, stealing, and committing adultery; they break all bounds and murder follows murder. Therefore the land mourns, and all who dwell in it languish."[3]

It is obvious that the lack of kindness pointed to in this passage can easily be found in a milieu of killing and stealing, etc. But how does this relate to swearing? Well, if an intensely insecure person, given to the vulgar extreme of profanity, has ever taken issue with you, you know for a fact that kindness is the farthest thing from his mind—and he goes out of his way to let you know that! Perhaps after he has reduced you to a smoldering pool he will turn his attention to solving the real problem at hand.

Yet we more frequently find that such a person appears to be more interested in demolishing your self-esteem—while propping up his own at your expense—than in solving true problems and making things work. There is, indeed, no kindness in *this* land.

Moreover, this passage of Scripture tells us that a distinctive feature of the situation in which these ugly bedfellows are to be found is in faithlessness. Is there a connection between a lack of faith and swearing? There is, but before we can see the connection, we must notice the relationship between profanity and anger—not merely the mundane kind of anger that flares up between people from time to time, but that deep-seated hostility which is directed at God and at others, as well as at oneself.

This anger of which we speak stems from a person's refusal, first of all, to accept that God knew what He was doing when He made him. When he says, "I was born at the wrong time into the wrong family with the wrong body and the wrong personality," he doesn't have to *get* mad. He's *already* there! (Remember the story of the recalcitrant pot that shook its fist in the face of the potter and railed out, "What are you doing? Don't make me this way!"[4])

Not that everyone is as dissatisfied with himself as all that (though you might be surprised to find how many really *are*). But when I feel valueless and fixate on any of these areas, whether it be my nose or my parents or my shyness, I end up saying, in effect, "God, You really blew it this time—and, by the way, *why* have You done this to me? If I were only different, maybe my life would be worth something."

This kind of thinking flies in the face of everything God has revealed about how He values us. He created us in His own image. That's pretty heavy when you stop to think about it. He says He loves us, has a meaningful plan for our lives, and doesn't want to spend eternity without us. (Read Isaiah 43:4-7.) That's great. But it's only for openers. When we sold ourselves into slavery to sin with all of its ramifications, He purchased us back! And His own Son was the asking price. And you know something? God thinks He got a good deal! Talk about VALUE! Because of God's act, human beings have become the most precious, most prized, most valuable beings in all creation, in the entire universe!

But you say, "It takes an awful lot of faith to believe all that!" And you're right. It *does* take a lot of faith to trust that God IS a good Creator and Redeemer and Shepherd. And exercising faith by taking God at His word is just what the people we're talking about are refusing to do.

If you're one of these people, you're upset with God for following "such an obviously defective plan" in making you, and frustrated with yourself at your basic powerlessness in terms of changing yourself, and resentful of others for the good they have received—all of which spells an ever-burning anger, a deep-seated rage, which often surfaces in the form of profanity.

We see, then, a sort of double-barreled relationship which encourages profane attitudes: When we fail to recognize by faith our value in God's estimation, we have something to swear about. When we fail to realize the value of others as God's creation—and as members of our own family—we feel free to curse them. That's what James alluded to when he asked,

How can we bless God while cursing His children?

Just as profanity can suggest unresolved anger in a person's life, it can also signify an attitude of pride. David writes: "For the sin of their mouths, the words of their lips, let them be trapped in their pride. For the cursing and lies which they utter, consume them in wrath . . . till they are no more."[5]

As in our youthful swearing we may have sought independence from our parents, so in our "mature" cursing of the Creator, we may discern a rebellious attempt to find independence from a God whom we feel has wronged us.

Only the prideful heart says, "God, I don't need You!" And if we allow this attitude to persist, we ultimately come to a point where we eliminate God from our thinking altogether. Notice how Scripture describes those who are "under the power of sin."[6]

Their throat is an open grave,
them they use their tongues to deceive.
The venom of asps is under their lips.
Their mouth is full of curses and bitter-
    ness.

Their feet are swift to shed blood,
in their paths are ruin and misery,
and the way of peace they do not know.
There is no fear of God before their eyes.

For the wicked boasts of the desires of his
     heart,
     and the man greedy for gain curses and
     renounces the Lord. . . .
All his thoughts are, 'There is no God.'
A psalmist must have had his own tongue
planted firmly in cheek when he described the
appearance and speech of the proud:
Pride is their necklace;
     violence covers them as a garment. . . .
They scoff and speak with malice;
     loftily they threaten oppression.
They set their mouths against the
     heavens.
     and their tongue struts through the
     earth.[8]
Have you ever met anyone like that? When
proceeding from a person of intelligence and
some polish, he or she can make profanity seem
almost profound, adding to an air of absolute
certainty and authority, letting you know that

anyone who disagrees must have his—uh, must have been born yesterday. But upon scrutiny, it is found that the profane person's words and ideas are so thoroughly lacking in substance that he may be seen to be no more than a conceited tongue strutting his way through life, singing his own praises.

Clearly, we have here a legitimate matter of concern, both for ourselves as Christians as well as for those who are not. But here, as in other areas, we must first look to our own house. It is a matter of concern all its own that so frequently we have to ask the question Should Christians really expect to be different from other people?

At least one non-Christian young woman on a public university campus in southern California thinks we should be different—especially in view of the "superior air" with which we carry ourselves. "They claim to be so much," she reflected. "Yet you see them involved in the same back-stabbing competition, the same petty selfishness, the same thoughtless disregard for others. They're like everyone else!"

"How does the bumper sticker 'CHRISTIANS AREN'T DIFFERENT—JUST

FORGIVEN' strike you?'' she was asked.

''It doesn't,'' she replied. ''It doesn't strike me at all. I'm so sick of 'Christian' bumper stickers and the little fish in the window. Don't put it on your *car*. *Live* it!''

Could we ask for a more scathing rebuke? How can the world believe that Christ is who He says He is when our lives, our very words, reveal suppressed insecurity, hidden resentment, submerged rage? (See John 17:21.)

Perhaps the most pertinent admonition by the apostles on the subject of what we should be comes from Paul: ''Therefore, my brothers, I implore you by God's mercy to offer your very selves to him: a living sacrifice, dedicated and fit for his acceptance, the worship offered by mind and heart. Adapt yourselves no longer to the pattern of this present world, but let your minds be remade and your whole nature thus transformed. Then you will be able to discern the will of God, and to know what is good, acceptable, and perfect.''[9]

We *should* expect to be different, and we have here a view that helps us answer more fully the question Different from what? We do not wish to identify ourselves with ''the profane'' as a class, but we may frequently, though unwittingly, identify ourselves with them by our more or less ''innocent'' profanity. In fact, profane people appear to be something less than the most joyful group around. It seems to be the perturbed person who tends to exhibit profane propensities.

Having gained understanding from our exposure to Scripture, it becomes clearer how some of the people we meet (even when they keep their mouths shut) are still mentally, spiritually, and more and more often, even physically profane. (See Psalm 62:3, 4.) Obviously, ''washing one's mouth out with soap'' is never going to touch that kind of pollution! There must be deeper answers.

Theory and philosophy are fine as far as they go, but how does that transformation which Paul refers to—the renewal of one's mind—come about? What can we constructively do to aid people who have enshrouded themselves in blue language? Perhaps we should direct these questions to *ourselves,* and in the answers gain some clues for our responses to others.

Do you find that your own attitudes—as expressed verbally—sometimes imply anger, frustration, negativeness, even hate? Have you ever offended good friends and even found it somewhat unpleasant to be around yourself? Do you *want* to change? If so, start with these specific steps.

Accept what your study of God's Word reveals to you concerning who you are and what God wants to be—for, in, and through you. Every truth in Scripture should have an important impact on the direction of our lives. *Knowing* and *understanding* are essential first steps toward a renewed mind. When we fail to seek the truth about the kind of person God is as revealed in Jesus, God Himself is forced to lament: "My people are destroyed for a lack of knowledge." "A people without understanding shall come to ruin."[10] The promise and affirmation of the psalmist "Thy word is a lamp to my feet and a light to my path"[11] is as modern today as when it was first penned.

You need to come to accept your own attitudes too. Talking out with God your negative thinking helps. Yelling at God in your anger is better than taking it out on another person, better even than taking it out on yourself. You can be free and authentic in your relationship with God. He can handle your frustrations. You'll soon not have to do so any longer. Why? Because such frankness with God helps you to open up your deepest feelings to yourself and to Him. This is the doorway to confession and agreement with God that you need Him to help you be a positive, creative person. God can deal with your anger and pain because He knows how you really feel even before you yourself know. (Moses went to God when in despair, and it was a secret of his success. See, for example, Numbers 11:10-15.) Besides, no one is as patient with us as is God!

Then, after you've had it out with God, determine to fill your mind with positive thoughts, and you will come to feel (eventually) as you have thought. In other words. . .

Believe that the facts of our origin and destiny are not merely dry, dusty theology, but living truth for your life—truth to affirm in the deep recesses of your mind on a moment-by-moment basis. Wisdom appropriates facts and makes them fruitful in life, believing that God can give it. So *ask* Him for wisdom! He's not hard to get along with. He has promised not to say, "What did you do with all I've already given you?'' James affirms that God will dispense wisdom "generously and without reproaching."[12]

This wisdom is essential for molding our attitudes and their frequently negative manifestations. "For where jealousy and selfish ambition exist, there will be disorder and every vile practice. But the wisdom from above is first pure, then peaceable, gentle, open to reason, full of mercy and good fruits, without uncertainty or insincerity."[13]

Obviously, we all need a *strong* measure of that wisdom in order to cope in an increasingly hectic and uncertain world. But what we often fail to realize is how the new attitudes which result from learning to see life through God's eyes free us from self-destructive behavior.

Create useful alternatives when the urge to swear strikes. There are many ways to express strong emotion without resorting to profanity. The English language has a wealth of words which describe properly and accurately the emotions of disgust, dismay, gladness, joy, sorrow, pain, longing, rage. A few minutes with a thesaurus turns up all sorts of words which are colorful without being offensive. Develop some alternative expletives which convey your thoughts and feelings accurately (assuming they are fit for the ''airwaves'' in the first place!).

Learn how to defuse other kinds of negativism too. When people center on all the terrible stuff of life, instead of the goodness, they get pushed out of shape when things don't go their way. Their expectations are so locked in that they've no room for surprises (not even *good* ones).

The Bible suggests a simple alternative: ''Above all, my brethren, do not swear, either by heaven or by earth or with any other oath, but let your yes be yes and your no be no, that you may not fall under condemnation.''[14]

But what should be heard from our mouths when Yes or No doesn't seem adequate? The Lord's brother goes on to say: ''Is any one among you suffering? Let him pray. Is any cheerful? Let him sing praise. Is any among you sick? Let him call for the elders of the church, and let them pray over him.''[15]

So there are certain things we can train our mouths to say that will help to cure the sickness at the heart level, where it really is centered. In this vein, James concludes, "Therefore confess your sins to one another, and pray for one another, that you may be healed."[16]

Determine to cultivate positive, constructive ideas consistently—even though doing so will require a good deal of attention and practice. Your subconscious mind may drag its feet in coming around even after you've changed the objective, conscious, chosen basis for evaluating the world and relating to events that happen to us. Because your subconscious can sabotage the best of intentions, be firm with your emotions.

It won't be easy to capture your feelings and make them your servants instead of the other way around, so don't become discouraged. As is true of any constructive change, old patterns don't disappear overnight. Hard as it is to believe at times, God's primary concern is centered in your growing desire to know Him as a friend. God is more aware than the most learned linguists of how culture has shaped the use of profanity, but He is far more interested in you than in your words. As you internalize His deep concern for you, your conversation will come to reflect the positive concepts of hope, caring, love, joy, patience, trust, and peace. The bitter roots of jealousy and selfishness, which tend to sprout in anger and flower in a bloom of vituperation, will be pulled out and destroyed. In their place will grow praise and righteousness—the sort of praise and righteousness *God* causes!

So far we've discussed how to understand and approach this area within your own life, and we've found some clues to help you relate to friends and associates. If you haven't already, you soon may find yourself in authority over others—in business, perhaps, but especially as parents and teachers. How can we most constructively deal with this problem in that context?

First, we need to remind ourselves that in dealing with "the problem" we can only deal with people, and there are certain ways we must not treat people. Our natural response to experiencing frustration over the use of profanity in our presence would be to condemn the user. Yet, this is a branch of the very tree we've been trying to dig out! Shaming someone for sinful behavior is not God's way of teaching. He never asks us to give up something simply to leave us nursing an aching emptiness. The story of the fellow who got rid of one devil only to have seven more come rushing illustrates that fact.[17]

"There is therefore now no condemnation for those who are in Christ Jesus."[18] We might also safely read, "There is no condemnation *in* those who are involved in a relationship with Christ Jesus." By condemning what we consider to be un-Christian, we might frighten the timid into behaving properly (for a time), while at the same time we incite the rebelliously independent to flaunt unacceptable behavior whenever possible. But those who come to Christ do so because they recognize that He loved them first,[19] while they were in the middle of sinful actions and attitudes.[20] It is only through affirmation and lovingly caring for someone who needs correction, that a *life*, as distinguished from mere *behavior*, can be changed.

Condemnation is counterproductive in even deeper ways. The utterance of swear words or other forms of profanity—especially in a subculture where it automatically carries with it a certain sense of having done the forbidden—

creates a corresponding sense of guilt in the speaker, a feeling intensified when he is upbraided. Those Christians who are sensitive to the way in which people respond to guilt realize that guilty feelings engender a sense of worthlessness which, in turn, fosters self-destructive behavior—even the *same kind* of behavior which we may have criticized! Perhaps this is one reason why Jesus advises "Condemn not, and you will not be condemned."[21]

Apparently, there is relatively little to be gained for people who are in authority in simply banning the use of offensive words and phrases. Forbidding them might decrease use in their presence (except during times of deliberate defiance), yet it will most likely increase use among the user's peers. It is not enough for a person to be told that certain language is intolerable. The root attitudes which cause the problem must be dealt with. As a person increasingly accepts the immensity of God's love for him or her *personally*, the sense of internal and external strife diminishes. The positiveness of joy drives out the impatience and anger, the hatred of self and the hatred of others. When a person innundates the mind with the positive material of life, negative material has no place to go but O-U-T! The individual who is in a growing relationship with Christ finds that his very attitudes are being healed.

If we demonstrate love and care for others by nurturing their growth rather than by trying to mold them after our own image through secular, human power, then we will see changes in those for whom we are responsible. We really need to live out the meaning of the words Paul wrote to the Galatians: "Brethren, if a man is overtaken in any trespass, you who are spiritual should restore him in a spirit of gentleness. Look to yourself, lest you too be tempted. Bear one another's burdens, and so fulfill the law of Christ."[22]

When you reject knowledge and understanding concerning yourself, your world, and the God who made you, you express a faithless attitude. Faithlessness almost always produces a feeling of resentment and anger and leads to a strong repudiation of what God has for you.

You need not *say* curses or even *feel* like cursing to have profane attitudes. The essential question to ask yourself is this: Are you disgruntled with life? You *are*, if hostility crowds out kindliness and motivates your actions. You *are*, if anxiety steals your confidence and rules your emotions. You *are*, if fretfulness and worry override peace. You *are*, if impatience supercedes patience and tolerance. You *are*, if insecurity robs you of the healthy self-concept God intends you should have. The heart that chafes, worries, forces, disbelieves, distrusts, squelches creativity, and harbors hostility is the heart which creates attitudes that cause you to be a purturbed person with profane propensities.

It's easy to get hung up on externals. It's a part of our human pride to want to grab onto our lives and the lives of others and try to force them into the shape which our own peculiar morality dictates. But only God offers real—inward—solutions to the real—inward—problem. When the inner man is addressed, the outward manifestations will reflect God's work of "inside-out" grace.

We'll still be in the world. We'll still have to take to heart Paul's admonition: "Be watchful, stand firm in your faith, be courageous, be strong. Let all that you do be done in love."[23]

We may still have to face verbal abuse. But

God's grace is sufficient for us. The God of all
comfort does not leave us comfortless.

> Like a sparrow in its flitting,
> Like a swallow in its flight,
> A curse that is causeless
> Does not alight.[24]

REFERENCES

1. Ecclesiastes 7:22, RSV.
2. James 3:7-10, NEB.
3. Hosea 4:1-3, RSV.
4. See Romans 9:20, 21; Isaiah 29:16; 64:8.
5. Psalm 59:12, 13, RSV.
6. Romans 3:9, RSV.
7. Romans 3:13-18; Psalm 10:3, 4, RSV.
8. Psalm 73:6-9, RSV.
9. Romans 12:1, 2, NEB.
10. Hosea 4:6, 14, RSV.
11. Psalm 119:105, RSV.
12. James 1:5, RSV.
13. James 3:6-18, RSV.
14. James 5:12; see also
    Matthew 5:34-37, RSV.
15. James 5:13, 14, RSV.
16. James 5:16, RSV.

17. Matthew 12:43-45.
18. Romans 8:1, RSV.
19. 1 John 4:19.
20. Romans 5:8.
21. Luke 6:37, RSV.
22. Galatians 6:1, 2, RSV.
23. 1 Corinthians 16:13, 14, RSV.
24. See Proverbs 26:2.